Print Handwriting Practice

250 Awesome Facts About Science, Animals, and History

SPRUCE BOOKS
A Sasquatch Books Imprint

Try it! First, trace over the letters. Then write them by yourself on the blank lines below.

Example:

More than one million Earths could fit inside the Sun.

More than one million Earths could fit inside the Sun.

More than one million Earths could fit inside the Sun.

Let's get started!

More than one million Earths could fit inside the Sun.

Koala fingerprints are almost identical to human fingerprints.

A shrimp's heart is located in its head.

Before Tokyo, Kyoto was the capital of Japan. The cities' names are made up of the same letters.

"Jingle Bells" was the first song played in space.

Each zebra's stripe pattern is unique, much like human fingerprints.

Coca-Cola was the first soft drink consumed in space.

NASA astronauts have a patch of Velcro sewn into their helmets so that they can scratch their noses.

Zambia and Zimbabwe are the only two countries in the world with names beginning with Z.

Humans sneeze at around 100 mph.

Archaeologists have found pots of honey in ancient Egyptian tombs that are still good to eat!

Knights usually began their training by the time they were seven years old.

A jiffy is a real unit of time. It is the time it takes light to travel one centimeter in a vacuum.

The blue whale is believed to be the largest animal to have ever lived on the planet.

Hippos have such thick skin that they are virtually bulletproof.

The English number four is spelled with the same number of letters as it describes.

There may be thousands, or even millions, of species we have not discovered yet.

The first marshmallows were made by the Ancient Egyptians.

Sharks don't have bones; their skeletons are made entirely of cartilage.

You are taller in the morning than you are at night.

Gold is created when neutron stars collide. A collision can produce enough gold to fill 200 Earths.

Most kangaroos are left-handed.

While floating on the ocean surface, sea otters hold hands to form large communities called rafts.

Cell phones used to be the size of bricks.

The world's tallest volcano, Mauna Loa in Hawaii, stands at 13,677 feet.

Henry III, the medieval King of England, once kept a polar bear as a pet at the Tower of London.

Alligators cannot live in salt water.

Bamboo can grow as much as three feet in one day.

James A. Garfield was the first left-handed president.

Oak trees are struck by lightning more often than any other tree species.

Starfish eat by turning their stomachs inside out and wrapping them around their food.

Helmets were not mandatory in the NFL until 1979.

Ancient Greek theater audiences would stamp their feet rather than clap to show appreciation.

Leonardo da Vinci could write with one hand while drawing with the other.

The longest bone in the human body is the femur (thighbone).

By age 60, the average person has lost half the taste buds on their tongue.

The world's biggest kite is nearly as wide as a football field.

A baby's eyes are almost adult size at birth, which is why they appear larger than the rest of their head.

When you blush, the lining of your stomach does too.

A 1 followed by 100 zeros is a googol. A 1 followed by a googol of zeros is a googolplex.

A group of meerkats is called a gang or mob.

The fear of getting peanut butter stuck on the roof of your mouth is called arachibutyrophobia.

Gummy bears are called jelly babies in England.

Early cannons could only be fired ten times an hour as their barrels had to cool down between shots.

Eating or licking a poison dart frog can cause almost instant death.

The name for the scent of old books is bibliosmia.

Defenders of castles dumped boiling water and hot sand on attackers from above.

Cats can see six times better at night than humans can.

Scorpions glow under black light.

The flag of the Philippines is flown upside down when the country is at war.

A bat can eat hundreds of mosquitoes in one night.

The pope cannot be an organ donor.

The first airplane flight lasted only 12 seconds.

Most sharks will drown if they stop swimming.

The average person produces enough saliva over their lifetime to fill two swimming pools.

The beard of a goat is called a goatee.

The Hawaiian word "aloha" means both hello and goodbye.

The shortest war in history lasted 38 minutes.

Penguins are the only birds that cannot fold their wings.

Castle floors were rarely swept; messes were often covered with straw and flowers.

Drinking salt water is more harmful than not drinking any water at all, as it dehydrates you.

Lightning can jump from an object to a person.

Most American car horns honk in the musical key of F.

Forest fires move more quickly uphill than downhill.

There are more kangaroos than people in Australia.

The United States Central Intelligence Agency once strapped cameras to pigeons trained to fly over enemy targets.

More than 85 percent of a Toyota Prius can be recycled.

Elephants are not able to jump.

Bird wings and human arms have the same bone structure, but birds can fly and humans can't.

Early hockey pucks were made from frozen cow dung.

A group of geese is called a gaggle when they're on the ground, and a skein when in flight.

More than 200 people could fit in the world's biggest igloo.

Carnivorous piranhas will clamp down on goats that fall into the water.

In castles, hay was used as toilet paper.

Chocolate-covered ants are considered a treat in Mexico.

In the Polish version of Scrabble, the letter Z is worth one point.

While a dozen is 12, a baker's dozen is 13.

The moon is a quarter of the size of Earth.

There are three times more chickens in the world than there are human beings.

Mummies have been found on every continent.

It's not possible to tickle yourself.

The blood of spiders is clear.

Antarctica was completely ice-free until about 34 million years ago.

Fish can taste not only in their mouths, but also all over their bodies.

Helium causes your voice to sound higher because sound travels more quickly through lighter air.

Argentina's president works in a building known as La Casa Rosada (The Pink House).

Animals can often sense natural disasters before humans do.

A cheetah can speed up faster than a race car.

Humans can nap with their eyes open.

Cows have best friends! They are calmer when they're with their buddy.

Penguins are drawn to the scent of rotting eggs.

In NASCAR races, four tires are changed and the car is refueled in fewer than 15 seconds.

Spiral staircases in castles often spiraled clockwise to disadvantage right-handed attackers.

Bat poop is called guano.

The human skull is made up of 22 bones.

Hippos cannot swim or float; they trot along the river or lake bed.

The Earth's core is hotter than the surface of the sun.

Military survival guides include instructions to eat insects if no other food is available.

Snow leopards keep warm by wrapping their long, fluffy tail around their bodies.

The only continent with no active volcanoes is Australia.

Iceland is the world's most peaceful country.

There are more caribou than people in Alaska.

Some fleas can jump more than 150 times their height.

Raindrops are shaped more like hamburger buns than teardrops.

The immortal jellyfish can live forever, growing to adulthood then reverting back to its baby state over and over.

A leech has at least 32 separate brains.

Praying mantis females often eat their mates, and babies sometimes eat their siblings.

Fireflies use their lights to communicate with each other. Different species have different flashing patterns.

The metal potassium explodes when it touches water.

The male narwhal's long, spiral tusk is actually a tooth growing out of its top lip.

Sea otter poop, called spraint, smells like herbal tea.

A chameleon's tongue is twice as long as its body.

Earth is the only planet in the solar system that has enough oxygen for fire to burn.

The Bible is the world's best-selling book of all time.

When a newt loses or damages a leg, it grows a new one.

By the age of six, a human's brain is already 90 percent of its adult size.

Skin is the body's largest organ.

Each of an ostrich's eyes is bigger than its brain.

Copper is a natural bacteria killer, which is why many public buildings have copper door handles.

Giant clams are big enough for a human child to fit inside.

Your heart beats 100,000 times a day and is the only muscle that never rests.

The Himalayas grow about 0.4 inches (1 cm) taller every year.

Handwriting started in Sumeria 5,000 years ago as a series of indentations in clay tablets.

Outer space is completely silent due to the lack of air to carry sound waves.

Around the world, lightning strikes 50 to 100 times every second.

Ancient horses were about the size of dogs.

Flamingo feathers get their pink color from the shrimp and algae the bird eats.

Limestone is made of seashells and can be found in places that were once covered by oceans.

Wood frogs freeze solid in the winter and thaw out in the spring.

Saturn changes color with the seasons. It looks blue in the winter and yellow in the summer.

A group of rhinoceros is known as a crash.

Australia is wider than Earth's moon.

Venus flytraps eat bugs to obtain nutrients that are not available in wetland soil.

When a dolphin sleeps, only half of its brain goes to sleep, allowing it to surface for air.

Sea stars don't have eyes; instead they have an eye spot on each arm that senses light.

Dolphins shed their skin once every two hours to keep them smooth and swimming efficiently.

A hummingbird's tongue is so long it coils inside its head.

The metal gallium will melt in your hands, because it turns from solid to liquid at 86°F (30°C).

Jellyfish have no heart, brain, blood, or skeleton. They are essentially floating stomachs.

It takes eight minutes for light from the sun to reach Earth.

The ocean floor is not flat; it has hills, mountains, plains, and the world's deepest valleys.

Mosquitoes use infrared light to find the best areas on an animal's body to draw blood.

Turtles can breathe through their butts.

Astronauts' bones become weaker the longer they stay in space.

Butterflies don't have tongues. They taste with their feet.

When iron is struck by lightning, it can become a lodestone—the only naturally occurring magnet.

Slugs are both male and female; they can fertilize their own eggs.

About 60 percent of the human brain is made of fat, making it the fattiest organ in the body.

Special feathers on owls' wings make their flight nearly silent, so they can surprise prey.

Thirty percent of the earth is covered in forests.

The colossal squid, the world's largest invertebrate, has eyes the size of basketballs.

A ladybug can eat up to 5,000 other bugs in one year.

The word "Sahara" means desert in Arabic, so the Sahara Desert is literally the desert desert.

One in every 2,000 babies is born with a tooth already in their mouth.

The Tasmanian devil is named after the frightening scream it makes when hunting at night.

Just as Earth experiences earthquakes, the moon experiences moonquakes.

Human eyes blink around 20 times a minute.

Eighty percent of the world's plants and animals are found in forests.

The giant squid has a doughnut-shaped brain. Everything it eats passes through the doughnut hole.

Astronauts get about 3 percent taller in space. Without gravity, their spines stretch.

The board game Mancala originated in ancient Africa.

Every number from 89 on has the letter N in its name.

Around 2,000 species of insects are considered edible for humans.

Grapes are the most popular fruit in the world.

An ocean sunfish sometimes floats on the water's surface to let birds pick parasites off of its body.

The world's oldest island is Madagascar.

The hottest temperature ever recorded was 134°F in Death Valley, California.

When underwater, a hippo can hold its breath for up to five minutes.

Winds inside a tornado can reach speeds of more than 300 mph.

Crickets and grasshoppers chirp differently depending on the temperature.

More than 18.5 percent of the world's most powerful earthquakes take place in Japan.

Switzerland's flag is perfectly square.

There are no lyrics in the Spanish national anthem.

The heat from the Big Bang still warms parts of the universe today.

Early Olympic athletes in Ancient Greece competed naked.

George Washington, the first United States president, never lived at the White House.

Cats have a third eyelid.

Your tongue has unique patterns just like your fingerprints.

The Ancient Romans used their pee as mouthwash.

People on the East Coast of the United States tend to prefer creamy peanut butter, while those on the West Coast prefer crunchy.

The tin can opener was invented 48 years after the tin can itself.

French fries were invented in Belgium.

The first recorded electric car was created in 1891.

The ostrich is the largest bird in the world. It typically stands around seven to nine feet tall.

Despite its name, the funny bone is actually a nerve.

The earthy smell after a heavy rainstorm is called petrichor.

Forty is the only number whose letters are in alphabetical order, F-O-R-T-Y.

A strand of spaghetti is called a spaghetto.

There is naturally a small amount of gold in human blood.

Cucumbers are made up of 96 percent water.

Ostriches are the only two-toed birds.

The Pacific Ocean covers 60 million square miles, making it the world's largest ocean.

The first food grown in space was potatoes.

Eating too many carrots can turn your skin orange.

Dolphins that are closely bonded may swim together in synchrony.

The blue in blue cheese is actually mold.

A five-minute shower uses 75 percent less water than a bath.

Snot is sticky because it collects debris that gets up your nose, turning into crumbly boogers.

In bowling, three strikes in a row is called a turkey.

The cheetah is the only big cat that cannot roar.

On Saturn, each season lasts about seven Earth years.

In Greece, showing your palm to someone is considered offensive.

Ice is lighter than water, which is why it floats.

LEGO bricks were originally created in Denmark.

Koalas sleep for up to 22 hours a day.

Sunsets on Mars appear blue.

There is no Roman numeral for the number zero.

Rabbits have almost twice as many taste buds as humans have.

China and India make up more than a third of the world's population.

The most common eye color in the world is brown.

Darker-colored popsicles tend to melt faster than lighter-colored ones.

Ninety-five percent of the universe is considered invisible.

Every snowflake is unique.

Dreams start when we enter REM (rapid-eye-movement) sleep, about 90 minutes after falling asleep.

Every night, hippos spend six hours eating an average of 88 pounds (40 kg) of grass.

A healthy person can survive only three days without water.

Sunlight helps your body produce vitamin D, which can make your bones and muscles stronger.

The ghost pepper is so hot that it can burn your skin.

South Africa's national anthem has five verses, sung in five different languages.

There are more lakes in Canada than in any other country.

It's not possible to sneeze with your eyes open.

Jaguars' eyes are more powerful at night than during the day, helping them to hunt in the dark.

Hamsters' teeth never stop growing.

More than 7,000 languages are spoken around the world.

Two peanut farmers have been elected president in the United States: Thomas Jefferson and Jimmy Carter.

The sun appears white when viewed from space.

Peru has more than 3,000 different kinds of potatoes.

The camel's long eyelashes help keep desert sand from blowing into its eyes.

The sun is almost perfectly round, unlike Earth.

The monarch butterfly weighs less than a paperclip.

The ocean is so big that more than 80 percent of it has not been explored.

Jupiter is more than twice the size of all the other planets in the solar system combined.

A polar bear can smell seals from 20 miles (32 km) away.

Moats were often used as castle garbage dumps and a place for emptying toilets.

A beaver can cut down 200 trees in one year.

There are more than 500 species of shark worldwide.

The Statue of Liberty's official name is Liberty Enlightening the World.

More than half of the oxygen we breathe comes from seaweed and plant plankton in the ocean.

Bats are the only mammals that can fly.

Some islands are human-made.

Venus takes 243 Earth days to rotate once but only 225 Earth days to orbit the sun!

An octopus has three hearts. Two pump blood to its gills, and one pumps it to the rest of its body.

A group of flamingos is called a flamboyance.

A single bolt of lightning contains enough energy to toast 100,000 slices of bread.

Pineapples take two years to grow.

Wombat poop is cube-shaped.

Handwriting is great exercise for your brain. It engages your memory, creativity, and cognitive functions.

Sloths can hold their breath longer than dolphins can.

A group of porcupines is called a prickle.

Bubblegum was originally gray. The pink color was added later.

Printed in China
Spruce Books with colophon is a registered trademark of Blue Star Press, LLC

10 9 8 7 6 5 4 3

The authorized representative in the EU for product safety and compliance is Authorised Rep Compliance Ltd., Ground Floor, 71 Lower Baggot Street, Dublin D02 P593, Ireland.
www.arccompliance.com

Editor: Brian Hurley
Production editor: Peggy Gannon
Cover illustration: GoodStudio
Cover photograph: © Katerina / Adobe Stock

Library of Congress Cataloging-in-Publication Data is available

ISBN: 978-1-63217-598-4

Sasquatch Books
1325 Fourth Avenue, Suite 1025
Seattle, WA 98101

SasquatchBooks.com